Gracie's Guide to Prevention of Suicide

Gracie's Mysteries
Super Spy Series

Angie Wilson
Illustrated by Ashley Teets

Headline Kids
an imprint of Headline Books, Inc.
Terra Alta, WV

Gracie's Guide to Prevention of Suicide

by Angie Wilson

illustrated by Ashley Teets

To order additional copies of this book, for book publishing information, or to contact the author:

Headline Books, Inc.
P.O. Box 52, Terra Alta, WV 26764
www.HeadlineBooks.com
Tel: 800-570-5951

Email: mybook@headlinebooks.com
Headline Kids is an imprint of Headline Books

www.AuthorAngieWilson.com

ISBN-13: 9781946664372

PRINTED IN THE UNITED STATES OF AMERICA

I would like to dedicate this book to my parents,
Buddy and Joyce Whitlow, for their nurturing love and
guidance. They provided hope and security through
faith in God throughout my childhood.

Being a friend is free. It's not always easy, but it's free. It's not always the popular choice, but it's free. It's just the right thing to do.

Gracie's BFF is Kenzie, and Kenzie's sister Ciara is her second-best friend. It's super cool because when she spends the night, she gets to hang out with both of them. The three of them like nothing more than sleeping on the floor in the middle of mountains of blankets and pillows, watching movies, and giggling until their mom makes them go to sleep. They have actually stayed up all night before!

Ciara is three years older than Gracie and Ciara, and most of the time they get along as well as you can expect where sisters are involved. But Gracie noticed that when Ciara entered middle school, she started pulling away from her and Kenzie. She no longer wanted to stay up late with them and giggle all night. Gracie's mom explained it was just part of growing up, which really bummed the two girls out.

So, now when Gracie spent the night, Ciara stayed on her phone. She was constantly texting, posting, and scrolling. She seemed to stay lost in the cyber world. Gracie and Kenzie had even stopped asking her to go anywhere with them. She just wasn't fun to be around anymore. It seemed she stayed angry a lot and was irritable. It was just too much drama!

The last time Gracie spent the night, Ciara was grounded because of bad grades, so she stayed locked up in her room the entire time. But still, no one thought this was anything to be worried about. It just seemed to be the norm for middle schoolers.

Yet, on Thanksgiving Day, when most of the world gathers with family and friends to give thanks, Ciara did not feel thankful. The weeks leading up to that day were terrible in her eyes. It all started with a text. Yes, something as simple as a text made her want to kill herself. You see there were these girls at school who always picked on her. They made fun of her hair, her clothes, and everything else. Ciara tried to brush it off as much as she could, but when you hear something over and over, sometimes it can sink in and feel very real.

There was a new guy at school, Kev, and he was the cutest! Every girl in the eighth grade wanted to be his girlfriend. Ciara couldn't believe it when he actually talked to her one day at lunch. She was ecstatic!

She noticed those girls giving her dirty looks. She tried to ignore it, but they wouldn't stop. She started finding notes in her locker, calling her ugly, fat, stupid and other bad names. One note said they were going to beat her up if she talked to Kev again. It really started to scare her, but Ciara didn't tell anyone. She threw the notes away and stayed quiet. She thought maybe if she ignored them, they would go away.

They didn't.

Things got worse. The girls started posting pictures of Ciara and making fun of her. They were always taking pictures at school and would try to catch Ciara looking bad- you know what I mean, we've all had those pictures where we don't look our best. This went on for months. Nothing seemed fun for Ciara anymore, all she wanted to do was crawl into her bed and sleep. She was sad all the time. Her parents noticed she wasn't herself, but then her parents had enough problems between the two of them, so it was hard to focus on anyone else. Her dad stayed gone a lot. Her mom tried talking to her a couple of times, but somehow Ciara convinced her nothing was wrong.

Ciara had good days and bad, but it seemed as time went on the bad outweighed the good. Her crush on Kev continued to grow, even though they didn't talk that much. When Thanksgiving rolled around, what should've been a wonderful family day ended up being a devastating day. Ciara was crushed when her dad moved out. He didn't even stay for dinner. She hid in her bedroom that night, with all intentions of going to bed early, but a text changed her life.

It was a group text from those girls. They sent a picture of one of them hugging Kev. It looked like the kind of hug between two people who are dating. The message was, "You were never pretty enough for him, he's mine now!"

Ciara's heart sank. This day had been horrendous. Actually, the past few months had been. She sat in the dark staring at the smile on Kev's face. She looked on social media, and sure enough, that picture popped up for the world to see. Kev even shared it, so it must be true. She threw her phone across the room and buried her head in her pillow. There was nothing good in her life right now. She had no friends. Her grades were terrible. Her parents had just split up. And, these girls had made her life absolutely miserable. She just didn't want to feel anymore—all her feelings hurt. She wanted all this pain to be over!

Sometime that night when her mom and Kenzie were asleep, Ciara tiptoed into the bathroom where she knew her mom kept her prescription pain medication. She grabbed a bottle of her mom's pills from the bathroom cabinet and swallowed them with a cup of water. At that moment, she realized what she had done was bad, and became terrified. She stumbled and fell as she walked down the hall, and yelled for her mom, who discovered the bottle still in her hand as she lay on the floor. Within minutes, emergency workers were there and rushed her to the hospital.

Gracie could not believe it the next morning when she received a call from Kenzie. Gracie and her mom rushed to the hospital to be with them. Ciara was going to live. Her stomach had been pumped of all the pills. Thankfully, her mom had found her in time.

Gracie cried as she sat in the waiting room with Kenzie. The two girls were shocked that Ciara would do such a thing. How did this happen? Why would she think of something so terrible as this? How did life get so bad that she wanted to end it? They used to be such close friends-what happened? They had more questions than answers.

Ciara's parents were beating themselves up about it as well. They blamed themselves because they were so focused on their own problems they didn't notice how bad life was for their daughter. They hung their heads as they thought of how self-centered they had been. Gracie and Kenzie were sad as well, as they wondered how they could've helped.

The next few weeks were the hardest in Gracie's life. She wanted to help Ciara and her whole family, but she didn't know where to start. Ciara and her family started counseling together. It was a good way for her to talk about her feelings, and help her face challenges in life. She also had sessions at school with the girls who were mean to her. The girls felt incredibly bad when they found out what had happened. They didn't become besties, but they did agree to leave Ciara alone.

Life was slowly getting better for Ciara. She realized Gracie and Kenzie were still pretty cool, and they started hanging out again. Their summer was planned with lots of sleep-overs, and a trip to the lake with Gracie's mom.

Ciara began to understand that life really wasn't as bad as it had seemed in that moment in her room. Sure, everyone has bad days, but nothing is ever so bad to do something that is so permanent that you cannot change it or do it over. A choice that means no more choices.

Gracie learned some really big lessons.

1. Life is never so bad to think of ending it. THINGS WILL GET BETTER!

2. When you see someone who seems depressed and who shuts everyone out, be a friend to him/her.

3. There will be bad days; you may even have a bunch of them together- but, keep your head up and realize everything will change with time.

4. Being a friend is free. It's not always easy, but it's free. It's not always the popular choice, but it's free. It's just the right thing to do.

Draw a trusted
adult in your life.

Who is this adult? ____________________

Always remember:

"Hatred brings conflict,
love brings friendship."

"Be kind to others,
be a friend."

Possible Trusted Adults

This is a list of possible trusted adults. There can be a chance of one or more of these people may not be trusted. Remember, a trusted adult is one who will not hurt you, nor have you do things that are wrong.

I	Y	E	R	P	G	X	L	A	P	I	C	N	I	R	P	C	V	R	Q	A	U	T	A
X	Y	T	E	G	W	C	D	S	B	A	Q	B	H	S	H	N	L	B	O	U	U	T	P
D	U	B	H	J	R	P	R	Y	D	Z	I	C	P	U	K	Y	K	P	Q	Z	E	N	Z
F	N	O	T	T	X	K	X	M	N	G	C	S	R	N	Y	R	E	H	T	O	M	S	T
X	C	M	O	V	A	P	D	U	N	L	O	C	Y	U	Q	X	A	X	K	V	F	C	O
I	L	A	M	E	P	E	R	M	L	O	H	D	L	T	Y	T	E	E	Q	N	X	H	Z
W	E	D	D	W	I	S	J	U	F	H	G	I	K	V	S	V	Y	U	H	U	R	O	M
O	H	F	N	T	E	J	T	T	E	R	I	W	U	R	V	P	L	X	Y	V	R	O	A
R	W	G	A	D	N	T	X	L	N	E	I	G	H	B	O	R	I	F	V	E	Y	L	F
R	M	H	R	H	L	E	P	V	R	O	B	E	B	O	M	I	S	K	T	L	K	C	G
E	G	W	G	R	X	E	R	D	F	J	N	P	N	H	T	M	Q	T	Y	P	S	O	W
C	E	F	G	Z	R	U	A	A	Y	E	O	V	H	D	R	R	I	V	P	T	D	U	C
I	Z	C	N	V	N	T	F	I	P	U	N	H	I	E	S	S	E	R	S	T	V	N	A
F	R	V	K	V	M	L	B	V	T	R	V	L	H	Q	Y	P	F	X	E	G	K	S	I
F	E	L	H	O	T	I	E	S	B	L	E	T	R	B	C	F	A	A	Q	I	C	E	K
O	H	I	G	G	Z	C	E	R	U	Y	A	T	A	K	R	J	C	R	M	V	Y	L	R
E	T	R	P	W	C	G	P	F	S	F	T	B	S	K	M	H	L	I	E	K	F	O	M
C	A	U	T	U	U	E	K	J	D	S	A	S	R	O	E	G	P	Z	F	N	Z	R	X
I	F	I	U	I	H	W	S	N	R	A	M	L	X	R	F	L	O	P	T	L	T	Y	N
L	C	N	P	E	Z	U	A	L	I	M	D	A	C	M	T	L	R	H	X	Z	I	T	Z
O	Z	X	J	S	B	R	H	V	V	B	F	G	C	H	P	P	C	R	U	O	O	Q	Q
P	Y	G	N	Z	G	W	V	E	E	M	Q	O	O	U	X	S	C	I	M	J	O	O	F
J	K	P	R	L	Z	W	I	G	R	O	L	D	E	R	S	I	S	T	E	R	E	D	W
Z	G	M	C	L	S	V	L	G	U	I	X	R	E	H	T	O	R	B	R	E	D	L	O

babysitter	neighbor	nurse	principal
church helper	foster parent	father	mother
older sister	grandmother	school	teacher
grandfather	police officer	counselor	uncle
older brother	bus driver	friends parent	aunt

Draw a picture of you being a friend to someone who is down.

Draw a way you can
help others be happy.

Crossword Puzzle

Accross

5 What is one thing the girls at school picked on Ciara about?

7 What is one thing Gracie, Kenzie, and Ciara enjoyed doing at the beginning of the story?

8 What did Ciara throw across the room when she saw the picture of Kev?

9 Who is the new guy at school?

Down

1 What is one thing Gracie, Kenzie, and Ciara planned for the summer?

2 What is one thing Ciara constantly did when Gracie spent the night after she entered middle school?

3 Why was Ciara grounded?

4 Gracie learned it's important to be what?

6 Who is Gracie's second best friend?

Find your way through the maze

Draw a picture to express how you feel inside.

Suicide

Most teens interviewed after making a suicide attempt say that they did it because they were trying to escape from a situation that seemed impossible to deal with or to get relief from really bad thoughts or feelings.

Warning Signs

There are often signs that someone may be thinking about or planning a suicide attempt. Here are some of them:

- talking about suicide or death in general
- talking about "going away"
- referring to things they "won't be needing," and giving away possessions
- talking about feeling hopeless or feeling guilty
- pulling away from friends or family and losing the desire to go out
- having no desire to take part in favorite things or activities
- having trouble concentrating or thinking clearly
- experiencing changes in eating or sleeping habits
- engaging in self-destructive behavior (drinking alcohol, taking drugs, or cutting, for example)

What if This Is You?

If you have been thinking about suicide, get help now. Depression is powerful. You can't wait and hope that your mood might improve. When a person has been feeling down for a long time, it's hard to step back and be objective.

Talk to someone you trust as soon as you can. If you can't talk to a parent, talk to a coach, a relative, a school counselor, a faith based leader, or a teacher. Call a suicide crisis line (such as 1-800-SUICIDE) or your local emergency number (911).

These toll-free lines are staffed 24 hours a day, 7 days a week by trained professionals who can help you without ever knowing your name or seeing your face. They are there to help you figure out how to work through tough situations.

What if It's Someone You Know?

It is always a good thing to start a conversation with someone you think may be considering suicide. It allows you to get help for the person, and just talking about it may help the person to feel less alone and more cared about and understood.

Talking things through also may give the person an opportunity to consider other solutions to problems. Most of the time, people who are considering suicide are willing to talk if someone asks them out of concern and care. Because people who are depressed are not as able to see answers as well as others, it can help to have someone work with them in coming up with at least one other way out of a bad situation.

Even if a friend or classmate swears you to secrecy, you must get help as soon as possible — your friend's life could depend on it. Someone who is seriously thinking about suicide may have sunk so deeply into an emotional hole that the person could be unable to recognize that he or she needs help. Tell an adult you trust as soon as possible.

Check out ALL of Gracie's Guide Books!